INVOCATION

AN ESSAY

❧

JENNIFER S. CHENG

INVOCATION

AN ESSAY

❦

JENNIFER S. CHENG

NEW MICHIGAN PRESS

TUCSON, ARIZONA

NEW MICHIGAN PRESS

DEPT OF ENGLISH, P. O. BOX 210067

UNIVERSITY OF ARIZONA

TUCSON, AZ 85721-0067

<http://newmichiganpress.com/nmp>

Orders and queries to nmp@thediagram.com.

ISBN 978-1-934832-27-1. FIRST PRINTING.

Printed in the United States of America.

Design by Ander Monson.

Cover art courtesy of the author.

CONTENTS

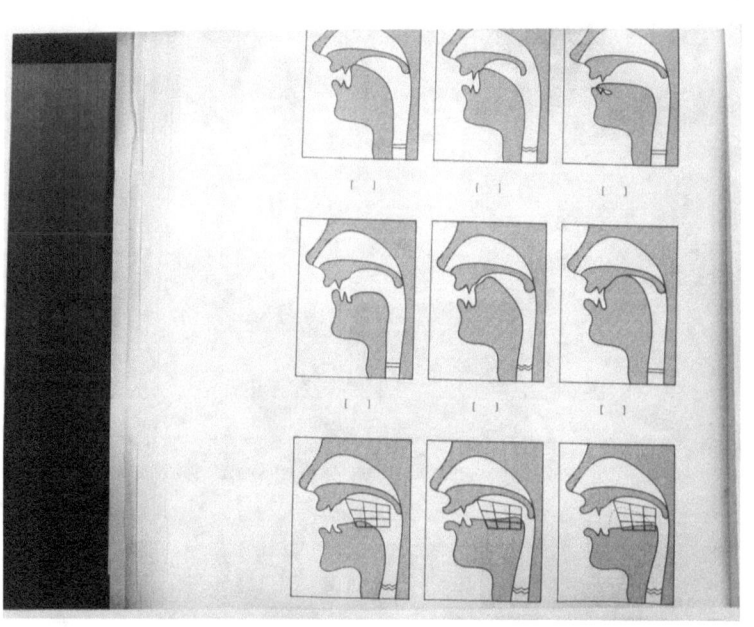

[ ]   [ ]   [ ]

[ ]   [ ]   [ ]

The world begins with a voice shut tightly, a closed throat.

When I speak, bitter molasses drips from my tongue
into still water basins.

A sound in water wants to find the surface, but depths
of water fill and push down. It happened one day that
the body tried to open its wings and found it could not
make a noise.

The speech act runs parallel to the act of assertion, of
proof. She aligns her feet under the table. Self-portrait
entitled *How to Part the Seas so the Sun Shines On It*.
Before moving to Iowa, she was often called *Loud Small
Girl*.

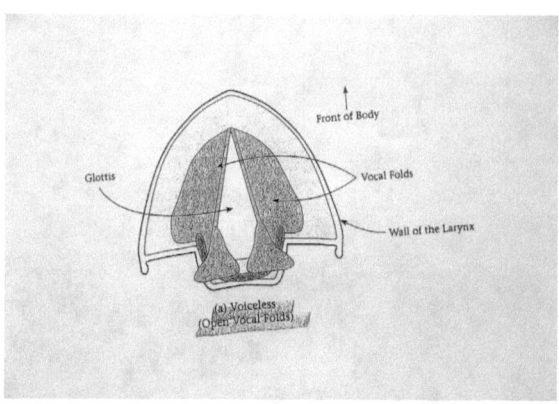

If it is true that the number of sentences coming out of my mouth is in direct relationship to my body in the world, then bones will become smaller, vacant. When I speak to the lady behind the counter or the person sitting next to me, I can never predict how my voice will sound: smooth, abrupt, flat, brittle, lingering. Now, it comes in tiny microscopic knots or large empty spaces, often then followed by *Did you say something?* or a continued conversation elsewhere around me. So that afterward in the darkness as I am riding home, I am looking out the window, thinking of octopi on the ocean floor and what they see at night.

8

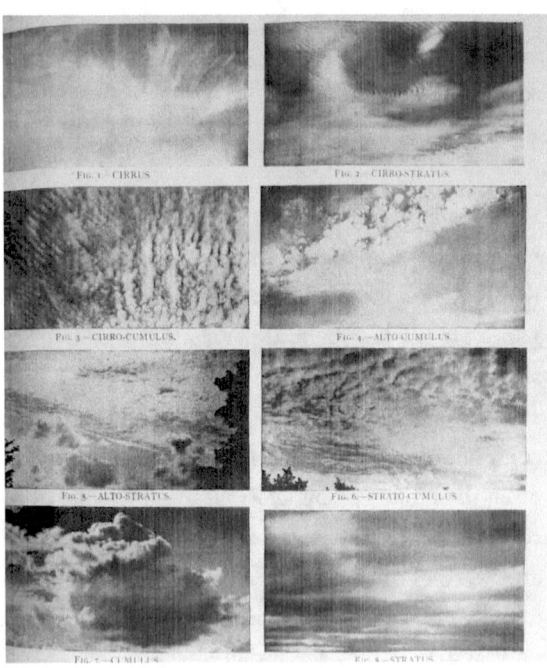

Fig. 1.—CIRRUS.   Fig. 2.—CIRRO-STRATUS.

Fig. 3.—CIRRO-CUMULUS.   Fig. 4.—ALTO-CUMULUS.

Fig. 5.—ALTO-STRATUS.   Fig. 6.—STRATO-CUMULUS.

Fig. 7.—CUMULUS.   Fig. 8.—STRATUS.

There are those who are born mute and those who develop levels of silence later in life. In hospitals there are patients who know what they want to say but cannot form the correct sounds, so it emerges as gibberish to the ears of the hearer—a kind of disconnect. And in other places, in secret places now hidden away, words are simply broken and language is splintered; sometimes there are children who stop speaking for inexplicable reasons, unknown even to them. And there is a kind of void, an absence, as if God was being flown away on a loose string in the sky.

(As if, at the same time, the world was hovering lower.)

The Breadth of an Utterance:

1. In a house crowded with other people, the night ends with her sitting on the floor in the shadow of a chair, eating slowly with a fork. It has to do with not knowing a way of being, of using language, a rhythm of body, which is to say it begins with uncertainty and ends with something darker.

2. When you are a child you are instructed to speak with a six-inch voice. This is to control the projection of words—a barrier that encloses your sound.

3. Eve, who was left with nothing to name and so wandered off alone into the moonless forest: wisps of lead-colored moss.

4. In a pool that is five feet deep, the water covers my head and I tiptoe-drift in the lukewarm encircling me, sun refracting shapes. I open my mouth, exhaling, vibrating, watching my muted sounds float tensely to the surface in little offspring bubbles.

Ghostly antics: Before women were unseen, they were unheard. They lived in silent rooms. Children who are repeatedly forgotten by those around them soon begin to slip. They find themselves in a place feeling like something of a foreigner. Illness: If you can't understand the ways of the people around you, like subtle shifts in movement. If you never felt that familiarity, and you are overwhelmed by the largeness, the lightness of the bodies surrounding you. Shut spaces: If the cavernous silence extends to the turning of the earth, where all gods and winged creatures drop over the edge.

As if Jonah had been left in the whale, and the tree
had withered on its own. As if a moth had fallen into a
glass jar and lay bare. As if the air were made of a thick,
viscous liquid and at the same time something empty.
As if it had all turned to salt. As if a great shape had
somewhere departed and in its place, a hole.

(7) Spectrograms of the vowels [i], [u], [ɑ]

equency (Hz)

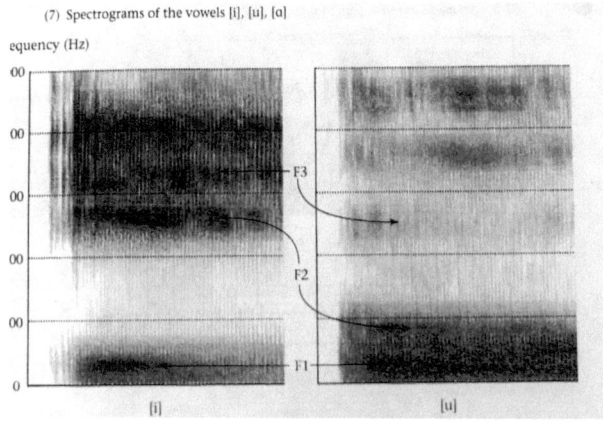

One sun-lit afternoon I fall asleep on my white bed, the thin curtain at the window completely still, and dream my mother is dead. I wake in my sheets, wet and crying, my body heavy and aching. I walk around the silent apartment aimlessly, the light still coming in through the window heavily. I call her on the phone but do not speak.

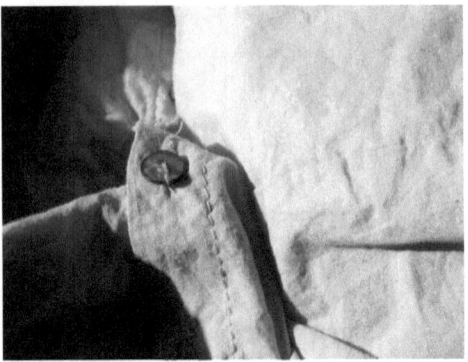

I think of small creatures beating softly in the darkness, of seahorses treading lightly on bright pebbles, wrapping their tails around blades of murky, shadowed grass.

Somewhere in the midnight, *a childhood across the sea,*
a black ocean constellation. Sometimes children stop
speaking because, lost in a stranger's land, they are left
with only their bodies. Without maps, they trace lines
of light on the palms of their hands.

Tucked into the folds of growing stalks and stems,
the only sound they hear is the silence of their bodies,
turned from frozen glass.

Before words, things were formless and void. Darkness was hovering.

(She walks through the grocery store while pushing a cart.
She waits in line.
She pays the cashier.
She washes vegetables, turning each leaf over.
She closes the refrigerator, sits at a table.
She turns on the water in the bathtub.
She looks at the tiles, blinking through droplets.
She puts on a shirt, brushes her teeth.
She turns off the light.
She curls on the bed.
She waits for her eyes to adjust to the dark.)

Sometimes the body reacts automatically and only later does the mind recognize and name what it is feeling. Sometimes the mind never recognizes so the body just continues. And amidst continuing, there are hollowed spaces in the corner between ligament and bone, the first step upward and the foot on the ground, my body touching the couch that is touching the floor that is touching the earth.

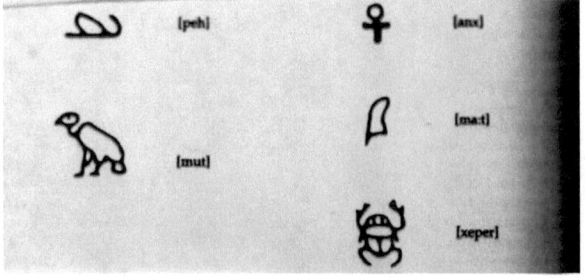

I make noises, stop, try to move my tongue, tongue over lips, tongue to the palate, mouth open, closed. Rain drips down from the bridge across the street.

And I wait as I sit riding on the bus, as I walk in and
out of buildings. I wait for lines of air to move upward
through the lungs, through ridges of tissue, oscillating.
Circulating out through the oral cavity. For light to
diffuse in through the curtains and catch on hanging
birds. For the excavated space following me everywhere
I go, just behind my head, to be filled with some sort of
shadow and the whisper of a name.

And somewhere just outside, on the doorstep of my house, even the saints do not wait; they lurk with lips sewn shut.

ACKNOWLEDGMENTS

Images, photographs, and diagrams are from various sources:

The diagram on page 1 is from ALGEO/PYLES. *Workbook for Algeo/Pyle's The Origins and Development of the English Language, 5th*, 5E. © 2005 Heinle/Arts & Sciences, a part of Cengage Learning, Inc. Reproduced by permission. www.cengage.com/permissions.

The photograph on page 4 is by Gideon Tsang. Used by permission.

The photographs on pages 5, 17, 23, and 35 were provided by my mother and father, James and Li-ma Cheng, and also my aunt Lulu Zheng.

The diagrams on pages 7, 19, and 30 are from *Language Files*, 10th ed., Ohio State University Press, 2007. Reproduced by permission.

The image on page 8 is from *Encyclopedia Britannica*, 11th ed., Vol. 6, Encyclopædia Britannica Company, 1910. (Public domain.)

The illustration on page 27 is from Lewis Carroll's *Alice's adventures under ground*, Macmillan and Co., 1886. (Public domain.)

I am grateful to Mary Ruefle and her Fall 2007 nonfiction workshop, Robin Hemley and his image essay assignment, Xu Xi, Patricia Foster, Maureen Robertson, April Freely, Spring Ulmer, and most of all Gary and my parents.

COLOPHON

Text is set in a digital version of Jenson, designed by
Robert Slimbach in 1996, and based on the work of
punchcutter, printer, and publisher Nicolas Jenson.

JENNIFER S. CHENG received her MFA from the Nonfiction Writing Program at the University of Iowa, and she holds a BA from Brown University. Her essays have appeared in *Seneca Review*, *The Collagist*, and the anthology *Fifty-Fifty: New Hong Kong Writing*. She is the recipient of a 2010-2011 Fulbright fellowship to Hong Kong, where she is currently researching and writing. Her home is in San Francisco.

✺

NEW MICHIGAN PRESS, based in Tucson, Arizona, prints poetry and prose chapbooks, especially work that transcends traditional genre. Together with DIAGRAM, NMP sponsors a yearly chapbook competition.

DIAGRAM, a journal of text, art, and schematic, is published bimonthly at THEDIAGRAM.COM. Periodic print anthologies are available from the New Michigan Press at NEWMICHIGANPRESS.COM/NMP.